LuvLock
Chain of Emotions

LuvLock
Chain of Emotions

Prince Ami

Copyright © 2018 by Prince Ami. All rights reserved. This book or any portion thereof may not be reproduced or used in any manner whatsoever without the express written permission of Prince Ami and Butterfly Typeface Publishing except for the use of brief quotations in a book review.

Printed in the United States of America

First Printing, 2018

ISBN: 978-1-947656-40-6

ISBN10: 1947656406

The Butterfly Typeface Publishing
PO BOX 56193
Little Rock Arkansas 72215

www.butterflytypeface.com

info@butterflytypeface.com

For my mother, Ms. Elizabeth Ann ...

"But this is a people robbed and spoiled;

they are all of them snared in holes,

and they are hid in prison houses:

they are for a prey, and none delivereth;

for a spoil, and none saith, Restore."

Isaiah 42:22.

Table of Contents

Poem: Signs 23
Essay: Thankful 24
Poem: Twinkle 26
Poem: The Fire of Commitment 26
Poem: The Essence of Beauty 28
Poem: The Spirit of The Wind 29
Poem: Entitled: Beyond Word's 30
Poem: Wishful Thinking 32
Poem: For Mama 33
Poem: 3 Words (Part 1) 34
Poem: 3 Words (Part 2) 36
Poem: Sick Fantasy 38
Poem: A Players Prayer 41
Speech: From Darkness to Light 42
Poem: History 46
Poem: See you later 47
Poem: Spring forward 49
Poem: Love Lock 50
Poem: When She Said Good-Bye 51
Poem: Real Love 52
Poem: Quit Playing 53

Poem: Beyond Ether 55
Poem: The Guy who couldn't leave and his unfortunate demise... 56
Poem: Air.. 58
Poem: When She's Away 60
Poem: The Takeover 61
Poem: Before you give my love away............................ 62
Poem: The reasons I do.. 63
Poem: Revenge 66
Poem: The Wonder of a Heart............................... 67
Poem: Sucker For Love... 68
Poem: Strength to Picture 69
Poem: Mental Souljah... 71
Poem: For Granted.. 73
Poem: Endurance.. 74
Poem: The Lost Heir... 78
Poem: A Vision Never Seen................................... 81
Poem: Growth Through Anger............................... 82
Poem: Theory of the Reasons as to why, She Refuses to Love 83
Poem: In My Rear-view... 84
Poem: Moving On 88
Poem: Building Blocks 90
Poem: Romeo's Lost Letter to Juliet 91
Poem: Picture Perfect 92
Poem: To Question Prophecy 93

Poem: Real Friends 94

Poem: If You're Alone 95

Poem: Awoken 96

Poem: My Goalz 98

Poem: Change Of Heart 100

Poem: A Day For Mothers 102

Poem: Kingston 104

Poem: The Worst 105

Poem: I'm Ready 107

Poem: Farewell 108

Poem: Complex Feelings 110

Poem: Something Special 112

Poem: Time 113

Foreword

To be confined is a horrible atrocity.

In death you have no worries. In prison worrying could drive you crazy.

I am a prisoner of my own thoughts. If I think good then no matter the physical circumstances in life, I will feel good!

It is what it is!

-Prince Ami

Acknowledgements

First off, all praise to the Most High Creator YAHWEH, for blessing me with the talent to write, and most of all I would like to Thank Elohim for bringing some of the most sweet and kind hearted women in the world into my life.

From my Mother Ms. Elizabeth Ann, I learned to be strong. She battled Rheumatoid Arthritis throughout my childhood but never did we miss a meal or did we lack the essentials. Mom, you were a Truly Virtuous Woman; thanks for all the good memories and being there for my bad ass. (lol)

Special thanks to my sister and all the sisters across the world that's keeping it *100* with all the family on lock. We love y'all and appreciate the letters, thoughts, holiday cards, prayers, answered calls and commissary. Without you and sisters like you, a lot of brothers would be knee deep in trouble. We appreciate the support.

To the women who inspired me to write this book, who brought light to my world when there was only darkness, there are no words to express the way that I feel. This book is dedicated to you and all the women across the world who haven't given up on their love that's locked...

To all my true brothers: Jizzle, thanks for the support bro, and to my brothers on Lock, K.P., Decky Boy, Dirt, Rico, Shoota, J Mack, Mur-Mur, Lil Toot, Dark Child, V.D.P. T-Bow., "Lord Unity Structure" and "Supreme Team" keep the faith, and remain strong.

Shalom,

-*Prince Ami*

Book 1

LuvLock

Poem: I Do

To the most beautiful woman in the world,
so delightful to behold, her eyes are the glow to my soul....
When it seems all has fell, she keeps me under control,
my balance and guide,
she has given me the knowledge to survive....
When I met you, there were certain things I doubted
but now I know are true, it's evident the sky is blue,
but what amazes me is how God made you....
Everything I need in one, all the virtues a woman should
possess are wrapped up in the character of you, no movie
or screenplay could capture the way you make me feel,
as if I'm floating into heavenly hills, I want this moment to
last forever, meaning you and me together, for better or
worse you'll always be my True Love....

LuvLock

Poem: Thoughts

In life you can endure so much, yet if it only be for this

moment that I might feel your touch,

nothing can bring me to tears,

or give me the power to face my fears,

than the beauty of blackness, so attractive she got my

heart racing rapidly, it's she that's got me hooked, such a

crook, I use to be a player now I'm playing by the book.

No need for persuasion as we begin to love, making

melodies with our bodies moving deep in harmony, betcha

like it: how I made you say "mercy me" beneath the sheets

I lick your feet, glide gently to your pretty pink,

For this woman here, I must admit I got much love, the

skies above be the witness to my testimony,

this little honey brown has got me thinking matrimony,

sweet chocolate I'm begging for you to come

LuvLock

and drop it on me,

just the thoughts I be thinking when I'm locked down

and lonely......

Poem: Valentine

There are a million ways,

for me to ask that you be mine....

If I could kiss your lips and squeeze your hips....

I would give you the most chocolaty gift,

unlike Hershey, I won't melt in your hand

and I promise to never be a minute man....

Well since I'm so sweet, I know you've had a busy week,

so today I'll rub and kiss your feet....

Like a taste of honey,

baby I wouldn't trade you for money....

You got that fire, you are everything I desire....

Boldness, bluntness, meekness and somewhere deep

inside lies treasure.....

Can't wait to explore your body,

I promise to be naughty,

LuvLock

I'll be gentle, every time you take a breath

the fire will rekindle....

There are so many ways to ask that you be mine,

I know I sound kind of silly

but baby would you please be my Valentine?

LuvLock

Poem: Signs

Jealousy is a sign of envy,

envy is a form of anger,

anger is a symptom of MADNESS.

One should not be jealous because they lack the essentials

they might want or aspire to have.

If any person has the energy to hate, they have the energy

to work and put forth the needed effort to succeed.

You only live once, but if you live the life of a hater

your days shall be few.....

Eat, drink, and be merry for tomorrow we die!

LuvLock

Essay: Thankful

There are many things I would like to give thanks for this this season and moment but no one are nobody could compare to the appreciation and thanks I have for you.

This season, I'm thankful that God brought us together. God could have given you to any man, that was in a better position than me, but when he considered love, he knew despite the circumstances we would make the perfect match. And for that I'm thankful this season.

This moment, it might sound crazy but I'm sure it was meant to be, it's like the stars aligned to bring us together, how else could I find an Angel, among all this danger.

Who would consider my soul while I'm oppressed, give me her heart and all her best, so at this moment I pray to have you always, because every moment with you is like a holiday.

In summary, there are many things I would like to give thanks for this season and this moment, but most of all I want to say thanks to you, because having you is truly a blessing and for that honor I am appreciative.

LuvLock

Poem: Love

Love is a feeling and desire

that cannot be explained by mere words....

Love is something no one should be deprived of....

Love is the tingling sensation you get in your chest

when you think about your significant other....

Love is the shiver in your spine when your mate is close,

Love is the burden to your heart

when your love is not near,

love is something that I hold very dear,

love is not something you can hear,

and most definitely not something you should fear,

it's the light beyond the darkness,

and the centerpiece to real happiness

Love!

Poem: Twinkle

Twinkle, no star in the galaxy could match your glow.

Twinkle, when I met you,

I was forever blinded by your natural beauty,

no other woman could meet your worth in value.

Because Twinkle, Twinkle you are more than a star

Juno couldn't match your shining light and no Eros or

Aphrodite couldn't match your love,

if Midas had the power to turn everything he touched into

gold, I know you could very well turn me into gold just by

smiling upon my trapped soul.

Twinkle.....

LuvLock

Poem: The Fire of Commitment

Love is an ongoing battle and a war within itself

In love u will endure hardships, strife, pain, bitterness,

jealousy and envy, but it's the very core and fabric of love

which enables us to endure all these things and stay

committed as one flesh.

Love is a two way street,

you must go up as well as go down

and when u can walk a mile with anyone,

u learn to feel their pain and that's what love is about

taking on the load of your significant other,

assisting her/him in carrying the load when they are at

their weakest and unable to do so for themselves.

Love is the basis and foundation of the true order of life

and the circle of humanity with man and woman as the

guardians of society!

LuvLock

Poem: The Essence of Beauty

Today I awoke to the appearance of the glorious Sun,

just beyond its horizon.

When I noticed it's fierce and beautiful hue,

I thought of you.

Maybe in time your glow will eclipse

its most radiant rays.

But all I request today, if nothing more, your lovely voice

and womanly touch forever more!

LuvLock

Poem: The Spirit of The Wind

As the wind blew,

One thing was certain to be true,

The everlasting burning fire shining in the eastern sky,

The burning desire I receive

when I look into your brown pretty eyes,

The way u got me hooked must be magic,

If it wasn't for love it would certainly be tragic,

As each day passes hope becomes much more

than a far-fetched possibility,

Beyond this horizon lies the key to reality,

You and me spiritually, mentally and physically,

In a union more powerful than the UN community,

Pulling strings to make the means as a family,

As the wind blows a kiss to matrimony,

Here is yet a revelation of my testimony.

LuvLock

Poem: Beyond Word's

There is something I must confess,

in this world that's such a mess,

you changed me baby you are the best.

With flying colors I would wear this ribbon

dedicated to the love of you,

in this world so corrupt I found something true,

that made me anew.

Like a moth to a flame, it's evident life won't be the same,

if I'm a Player then you are the Game

Let's be real it would take a speech

to explain the way that we feel,

it's like walking into heavenly hills,

as you wake this is something you can trust is real.

Like the arteries in your heart,

we should never be apart, as we play this card,

I hope fate is on our side, that the moment will come that

you will be my bride, on the clouds of Jupiter we shall soar,

LuvLock

to the great sky's and beyond

I'll be yours forever more!

Poem: Wishful Thinking

Even if there is no room

In this eerie pit of doom

To put a tree, and place you under

There is still no wonder;

How you bring me joy,

If Santa could bring me any little toy

I would trade them all just for you,

And I hope you would do the same for me too!

Wishful thinking.

LuvLock

Poem: For Mama

When I was sad it was you who brought me mental joy.

There are no words to express the wonders you've done to raise me from a boy to a man.

This couldn't have been a part of your plan.

For me to be captive a victim to my own actions.

Trapped inside the walls of Uncle Thomas pen, it seems drastic choices has me voiceless.

A prisoner of a larger war between race and creed.

What was once an abandoned seed.

Found breath among demon's, air became reasons to excel against all odds to make mama proud.

To the woman who bore me, from her flesh I became a knight to carry our name.

For Mama

LuvLock

Poem: 3 Words (Part 1)

I really can't stand the thought of being alone,

every man needs a woman to call his own.

How could she turn this fractured soul,

into a happy dwelling? Ain't no telling.

It's a miracle, she was sent from heaven,

when the wind blew she was there for me.

To shelter me because, she cares for me.

In the event the shipwrecks, she would drown with me.

If the feds kicks in our front door, you'll be the first to start

bursting, shooting, screaming,

"You ain't taking my Almond Joy."

She'll go toe to toe with any hoe,

that tries to fuck with her Butter-finger.

She knows I'll go crazy about my Cocoa Puffs and start a

war about my Reese's Pieces.

I've had my share of chocolate candies,

that was fine and dainty.

Prince Ami | 34

LuvLock

But you're the best in the cookie jar, I dedicate this poem

to you, you already knew, I love you boo!

Poem: 3 Words (Part 2)

If to say them 3 words loudly, makes me less than a man,

then I'm folding my hand, I'm leaving this game,

could care less about their feelings,

or what they perceive.

See it's all about you, all about I,

all about us for the rest of our lives.

Fulfilling our vows, weathering storms

and winning the trials.

When we grow old, we'll look back and smile,

and if you should leave before I do.

I pray Dear Lord, HE takes me too,

cause I wouldn't want to live without you.

This life wouldn't seem real without you,

all these feelings held up inside.

I've been at war all of my life, I finally found peace,

when I found you.

LuvLock

One thing I know, has got to be true, that if the sky is certainly blue, then girl you are the Glorious Moon!

LuvLock

Poem: Sick Fantasy

It's a ongoing warfare, I got this tick in my heart, that's a

pain in my side like a snake in the dark.

Tina so foolish, asking

"What's love got to do with it, if it's a art."

Then this vivid illustration,

is a portrait of all mankind's frustrations.

Time wasted chasing, cute faces, slim waists, fat ass's the

measurements are like math equations.

Maybe I should just capture Cupid, hold him hostage.

Pour a little bit of his secret potion, in her drink at the

movies, take one of his arrows aim

and shoot her in the heart.

Is this enough power to ensure, that only death will do us

part? Maybe I need to reconsider, the fact that I'll never

be too old to read some literature.

LuvLock

Thought I had you figured out, that I would conquer you, but you've captured me, now there is nothing left but this fantasy....

Book 2

Poem: A Players Prayer

To me it seems that life is just not fair.

The woman in whom I should treat with gentle care.

I abuse, neglect and often ignore, maybe its because of my

complex or the fact I was born poor.

I should have been a man, I should have done more, to

protect you from harm, instead I become

the source to the fatal storm.

I lost you because of my fear, blind to the power within my

own ear, I failed to listen and hear.

Time and time again you accepted me back,

I should have done better, maybe we would still be

together. Now I'm in deep thought as I pray,

God bring her back, before I lay.

I place my trust in side of you, if there be some way you

might bring Her back, I promise I'll never slack.

A Player's Prayer

Speech: From Darkness to Light

How can a person that has never been sick minister unto the sick? It's impossible for a person that's never been sick to genuinely understand the struggles, pain, and suffering of sick people.

For I was once sick, I have been lost, blinded in the midst of a world of corruption.

When children in the inner chocolate cities, think about whom they want to be or what they want to be in life; they don't picture themselves as cops, lawyers, judges, teachers, preachers and law-abiding citizens. They picture themselves as the people of their environment; as pimps, drug dealers, thieves, robbers, hustlers and murders, because these are the people they see when they look out the window. When they turn on the T.V. (M.T.V., the local news and other major networks who publicize these atrocities) they see images of people who aren't out right condemned. Some networks even motivate and encourage deceitful, malice, lustful, and wicked activity among minority people within America. I am not speaking on physical sickness, but mental sickness, sickness of the mind.

When the children of today, hear the word on Sunday it's only for a moment, because when they leave church they return to the same conditions; the abusive father or mother, the alcoholic step-dad, the empty house, no food in the refrigerator, no a/c in the summer, and no heat in the winter. The children (The Future) can't see the promise land because of the rain of troubles and thunderstorms which most suffer at no fault of their own.

So that's when depression, covetousness, envy, anger and lust begin to seep into the minds of our children. Our little brothers and sisters are being hit with a sense of doom and worthlessness at birth; not through the choices of life but at birth our children are conquered by a sense of doom, depression and loneliness.

How can a person that's never suffered these things, understand and consider the soul of these people? And why won't the children listen to the leaders of the fore-front of today?

I will answer that question. They won't listen because the leaders want to give the message without the testimony. See it's easier to tell someone how you *think* they should live, behave and act; but when you have never experienced what these children have been through you don't understand the reality of the difficult process of changing.

So when the children see these so called leaders on T.V. programs, at schools and other social events, they hear the message loud and clear and believe. Most of these children want to change for the better, and excel down the road to progress, but don't know how, because they haven't heard the testimony, the breakthrough of how God can bring you from Darkness to Light.

The message is given but the instructions (The Testimony) which is necessary to carry out the message is never heard by these children.

That's why the creator chose men and women like me and you. People who have been in lowly positions, who have been lost, who have been blinded by this world of corruption, who have come from Darkness to Light and exalted themselves from their lowly positions above (but not before) all mankind to go and minister the word unto the world.

LuvLock

For the messiah came not to heal those who are well, but the sick! That's why he chose company with people like me and you, the lost sheep. For who would be best to lead the lost, then those who were lost themselves, from Darkness to Light.

LuvLock

Poem: History

Every holiday I would want to be with you, even on Easter,

If you were a basket, oh how I would love to lay my eggs

You are so sweet, no chocolate candy

can compare to the taste of you,

Let's be honest I would love to be inside of you, yet if

nothing more be possible this Easter,

to hear your voice would bring me cheer.

With you I find inspiration to face my fears,

Today this golden egg, will represent our golden years

Me and you like Jack and Jill on this hill, we'll place our

name and throughout the generations our love will

become fame....

Poem: See You Later

I'll be your sex addict,

placing my hands on you will be nature pure habit

Neck, back, tits, and clit, there is no place on you baby,

that I want lick

I'll go a little deeper, bring out the freak in you

that's of late been a sleeper

Now that your love is free, I'll give you all of me

When I was locked, you endured like the hand on the clock

Never missing a beat, that's why I adore you

from your head to your feet

3 Times a day I'll give you a treat,

on every other Friday I'll give you my check,

this is something you can certainly bet,

count on me I'll always be there,

when all else fails I will always care.

LuvLock

No matter what you do, I'll see you through, from the bed to the jet, you'll always fly high, and I will always see you later because only death could tell us bye.....

Poem: Spring Forward

Talking about springing forward, while I'm laid back cooped up in this chicken pen, jotting fancy lines about my baby, how she'll always be my lady,
should she leave I might go crazy.
I think of her, me loving her, she licking me, me licking her, our tongues will play a game of tug of war, I'll pin you down and fuck you rough,
bend ya back, want cut you slack!
I think this is how I'll pay you back, you held me down, you stayed around, you held the throne, for you I write this very song, for you I'll give my every dime, just thoughts trapped inside my mind while I'm waiting doing time.

Poem: Love Lock

On a quest to find, a rare beauty that's one of a kind, this woman has heart, soul, body and mind
Tender lips her words are choice, a silky voice, that makes me melt, a love like this I have never felt,
At night I close my eyes, there is no surprise she'll be there, to comfort me, the woman in whom I search to find, has made a home inside my heart and mind.
Separated by thousands of miles, our love traveled the distance we became one over a late night conversation. Through daily communication we became infatuated with the idea of Bonnie and Clyde, me being your Husband and you being my Bride.
When the wait is over, I just wish and hope you'll still be by my side.

Poem: When She Said Good-Bye

Broken bottle tears,

The pain and agony of being alone so many years.

Despite the fact of our separation,

we kept in communication

As friends, I began to rethink the idea of being more,

remember how I use to adore

The things you did, to make me smile

with the cheer of a kid

Maybe I deserve better, maybe I should forget the thought

of us being together

Through sickness and health, until death do us part, wasn't

those the words we exchanged from our heart

I guess things change, but I surely want cry, I'm a man I

can accept the choice of you saying good-bye

LuvLock

Poem: Real Love

If you're in search for real love,

heaven sent to bring you into higher elevations

Mentally, spiritually, physically and financially

Something like a diamond,

consisting of the most finest qualities and attributes

Real love, ain't hard to find if it's not evident anywhere

else, close your eyes and you should find a love more

powerful than any of them all

A love for self, no greater treasure to possess and treasure

Than the beauty in you, just imagine if you didn't love

yourself who else would?

No Man, Woman, Thing or creature could imitate or

replace the love we should have for self, when all else fails

this is the power which enables us to endure, true and

pure

REAL LOVE for Self!

LuvLock

Poem: Quit Playing
For: Rachelle

She attempts to paint me,

Talking bout I'm not saintly

How dare you judge, with envy she holds onto a grudge

As if I'd conspire with a love that's a foe, how many times

have I had to pick my heart from the floor

Treat me as if I'm trash, unabashed if I'm such a dirty nicca

why bother or figure, attempt to make me

as your partner and lover

I guess the things that you say are really games, that's how

you have the most fun by using silly names

Aren't we adults, we should be in a palace

on the far side of the atlas

Where the trees are always green, and the waters are

always blue, this is supposed to be me and you!

LuvLock

Poem: Selfish

Am I selfish? I considered me when no one else would

When I considered you, you never understood

I gave in and I gave out, but I never gave up

I believed in you, I considered you I cared for you

I should have knew better than to neglect myself,

like you would consider me

I know better now and you want get me again,

because I'll be my best lover and my best friend

that's a fact even I can trust until the very end!

Poem: Beyond Either

Just because they captured my mind,

does it mean I'll let them conquer my soul

Captured me whole Continued Strong

on every denied appeal date

Either lifting weights, playing Spade's to hustle

Imagine us on a dinner date

Eating shrimp, lobsters and steaks

Making sure you eat your extra servings

Because I love your thick hips, plush lips

Tight gut, and fat butt

Makes me want to say "Oh my Gosh".

A country boy and city girl

Give me you your love, and I'll give the world

Let the truth be told,

"nothing can compare to the power of love within the

black soul".

LuvLock

Poem: The Guy Who Couldn't Leave & His Unfortunate Demise

Love can't be magic

In time I have learned it can be certainly tragic.

Like a needle to the heart

I should have knew from the start.

That a girl like you would make a fool of me

Isn't she?

The woman of my dreams

High yellow, honey brown cream.

I should have walked away, every time I tried my heart

refused to leave, with you it will always stay.

You became a sickness to my bones

I'm sure it would be best to leave you alone.

I should have packed my box and kicked rock's.

A long time ago now that option is not so.

You've rendered me useless with your constant nagging

LuvLock

I can't seem to think because you're always haggling.

Should I not die of love,

I'm pretty sure you'll be the reason

My family will have to prepare my burial

sometime this season.

LuvLock

Poem: Air

I need you, you're the fire in my eyes

The Queen in whom lies my desire.

The highest of the highs

Your reign is above the skies.

With you there is no surprise.

Two, four, seven, three-six-five

With you I know I'll survive, you are the breath which

keeps me alive.

My air

Book 3

LuvLock

Poem: When She's Away

From outer space, to the inner earth I scream, I'll be your Angel, shield, sword and guide when faced with danger, to you I want be a stranger,

To every step you take, I want be far away, I'll always be near to show you the way, in every way, always, sun up to sundown, Monday to Sunday, no day will be a bad day

The only days that won't be bliss, are the days you're gone, these are the days I miss,

Your smile, fragrance, touch, voice and eye's

Neck, back, clit and thighs.

When She's away

LuvLock

Poem: The Takeover

Tell me this would you figure,

27 years now I'm a self-made figure

Numbers and equations had to be added, the school of

hard knocks I have finally passed it

My mom's looking down her child has finally dad it,

my sister so proud that her brother finally had it

Left the nuance the noose is now loose,

A young Black King here's the fruit who needs juice?

Stupid infidels the lion rules the jungle,

you best be good I mean you better be humble

When I say silence I mean don't even mumble,

when I speak up it's like a big rumble!

LuvLock

Poem: Before You Give My Love Away

If you're thinking about giving my love away,

I want you to reconsider, all the time invested,

the memories we've shared, the trials endured.

When no one else cared, I was there, when you lost hope,

I became your shelter to weather the storm, on the day's

you thought you wouldn't make it I brought you back to

the norm, just something to consider before you give my

love away, who else will consider you if you walk away?

Poem: The Reasons I Do

The reasons I do, the reasons I do sacrifice my body as a

living testament of my love for you,

is because you are the reasons behind my mental joy.

Just as my memories begin to fade, your love revives me

so that I want pass away, renewing me daily

you are my living wishing well.

When I look into your eyes, I see the utmost respect a

woman can have for a man in you. And to know that you

feel this special way for me increases

the power of love I have for you.

When you speak, the sun seems to shine a little brighter

and when you walk my heart begins to beat a little faster,

because to know you are near

is the most wonderful thing to hear.

The reasons I do, the reasons I do, love you so.

Cannot be valued by a numerical equation; as the sands of

the seashore are innumerable so is my love for you.

LuvLock

I love your cheekbones, dark eyes, and your elegant skin tone you are so beautiful to me. It's not just your outer appearance which amazes me; it is the very essence of your inner-core which attracts me to you. The unseen fabrics of your heart which can be as boisterous as a lion or as gentle as a precious girl. It's hard to imagine a world in which I wouldn't, because for you there's this guarantee "I Do".

Poem: Locksmith

Dedicated To: Stephanie

As it appeared to me in a vision of simplicity

The key to reality only you could set me free mentally

Locksmith, no other woman in heaven or earth

could catch my drift

Yet you understood all the mechanisms within,

to set me free time and time again

You offered me freedom you set me free,

to my heart God must have giving you a key.

Locksmith

LuvLock

Poem: Revenge

Dedicated to: My unfortunate Destiny

One bullet to spare, without a care in this world.

Should I aim at my head or bust back at destiny?

Why does she keep stressing me?

Poverty stricken grief bared, crazy how I endured.

Many wondered how, a kid like this could survive

Against all odds he would thrive.

Some sourly say it shouldn't be,

how he should have died before twenty three.

Now he rise, as a newborn man. One bullet to spare, how

could he care? In this world that's so unfair.

I figured since she wants me dead,

I'll live and let be instead!

LuvLock

Poem: The Wonder of a Heart

To my heart, who caused it to grow

When it was damaged she nurtured it so

Our rhythm found it's sync

This is the beginning of true love don't you think?

Like the bird who couldn't fly or the deer who couldn't run

I grew to know, without you life just wouldn't be fun.

Poem: Sucker For Love

Sometimes I feel as if I could give her the world,

and she would say "No baby I requested the other planet",

We're supposed to be in a partnership

but she has me feeling like a servant damn it.

Even when it seems I can't stand it I run back for more,

as the tears form in my eye's

it's like this is what she adore!

To see me humble and meek, placing my head at her feet.

Bipolar isn't the word, what we have is so absurd.

Poem: Strength to Picture

I'll paint this picture to describe the way I feel,

viewers be advised to some this might be too real.

That those of my complex,

can hate with no remorse or regret.

Kill for any reason, my hopes

and ambitions these are demons.

Claiming they are my kin,

but hey there is no need to pretend.

The lines are drawn as feud's are born,

mortal men die by an oath sworn.

As the police swarm to secure the scene

as suspects flee without a care, another brother is

sacrificed within this ongoing warfare.

Between Abel and Cain, it seems some things never

change nicca killed a nicca again.

And they wonder why I'm speechless,

if I open my mouth I'll be victimized by leeches.

LuvLock

Mentally, physically no matter how much they get to me,

I'll continue to do better for me and my community.

LuvLock

Poem: Mental Souljah

Dedicated to: The Power of Mind

In the depths of my mind I dream of a place

as of late has been hard to find.

No one can understand my pain,

without hope what is there to gain?

Broken bottle dream's is all I have,

what ifs and maybes hunt me daily.

But if I close my eyes I'll be free, in a different world,

where there lies peace

maybe this could be the place for me.

Yet each day I awake to the same misery,

a reflection of my mistakes

throughout the course of history.

Forever etched within my mind,

I feel maybe I'll be better off blind!

LuvLock

Why see? If only darkness lie ahead,

I've contemplated suicide would this world be happy

if I was dead?

But never with a heart of leather I endure, despite these

shackles and chains I've managed to remain pure, and this

anger's my foes I'm sure.

Poem: For Granted

Don't take me for granted

tomorrow is never promised and who's to say that things

might not turn out a different way.

Who needs flowers when they are gone?

As if I could smell there scent from the grave you miss me

now, what about while here,

you never brought me gifts you seldom brought me cheer.

I was so disappointed as I fought my battle with death,

I thought this would bring us closer

but you only thought of yourself.

So I prayed that in the hereafter

we could rewrite life's chapter

That we'd be immortalized beyond the vast skies where

you want take me for granted, in Heaven's garden our

Root's will be planted, only if you'd promise to never take

me for granted!

LuvLock

Poem: Endurance

Dedicated To: All the Black, Brown, Caramel and Yellow Boys and Girls in the Hood whom Society said wouldn't be SHIT!

With a fist of steel and mind of rigor

I lash out with angry words and deeds to describe my pain

From birth I've been filled with the hate of a wounded warrior

My scars are unique, yet who can picture the pain within?

The hurt, anger and frustration that I feel

Without a silver spoon, teacher's cared less if I learned

As I continued to fail they continue to pass me on

Should I blame society or the simplicity of my own mind

Refusing to use my most precious gift

The power of mind to know yet refuse to do

To consider right yet still do wrong

Tell me how can you nurture a seed that's poisoned to be

damned if it grows it will wither in the lack of equality

LuvLock

In Autumn the leaves will fade, and what was once this

flower's shade will be its doom

For the sun will rise and burn it soon, even as the light

shines and the other creature's and plant's succumb

The Gladiolus somehow continues to blossom and Bloom!

Endurance

LuvLock

Poem: Numbers Don't Lie

Number's don't lie, so neither will I.

Take a seat enjoy the ride

as we begin this voyage unto the dark side.

In the streets kids play, on the corner a pusher slings,

a harlot whores and a addict lays.

In the window this is the place my mother often came to

pray, even as she knelt another pays in life and limb, oh

why must life be this way?

Take off those shades and lie down that herb,

you'll need a natural high to endure this pain,

either we didn't have meats or we couldn't afford sweets,

so when we wanted candy it came through theft,

little boys and girls so hungry they had no resort

but to steal from the store down the street, no father

single mother no one else cared if we eat!

LuvLock

How can you envy a child, who wanders the world with a forced smile, wanting to do right yet it seems only wrong follows, after a while they don't bother
I'm very sad numbers don't lie, so neither will I, 7 out of 10 black, brown or yellow skin locked within, confined in a system of repetitive sins, struggling to be rich we only find success in death, may I ask you this question,
What will you do to help? Soon there won't be any Left!
Black Man....

LuvLock

Poem: The Lost Heir

Through the good times and bad times

a quality like yours is hard to find,

as rare as a hidden treasure we make each other better

The chemistry we have cannot be recreated in a lab

The way I feel for you is natural, just as night awaits day,

the moment I met you

I knew you would take my heart away

We blossomed through rocky hills and thorns,

and from your womb a heir should form

No other moment could compare to the sight of our child,

in my sleep I picture his smile

To die thrice would be an ease,

if only I could see my unborn seed

When we lost him I lost you, the most beautiful woman

I ever knew

LuvLock

Beside my mother, to give me the world would never be enough to replace the sight of your smile or the unfortunate death of my unborn child!

Book 4

Poem: A Vision Never Seen

Dedicated To: My Hero's Jacob (Israel), Huey P. Newton, Malcolm X, & Amaru Shakur

To love or hate, perceive and think, acknowledge and grow, pass the sorrows of life's Woes

A vision never seen, is it a dream or a terror, to move through life's barriers

As is the sight of wind you can feel but not see, even I wonder how this could be

As the dusk moves through the hourglass, I ponder how such things could come to pass

That death increase, yet still there is no peace

If I bear the cross and carry it so for all the atrocities committed across the globe, will they remember my deed in text and creed?

Or shall I be forgotten, a vision never seen!

Poem: Growth Through Anger

Dedicated To: Lacole

Baby give me one minute to explain,

you rarely listen and this has driven us both insane!

We fuss and fight, about the things we both know we

shouldn't, but doesn't this drive us more,

to mend and grow?

We live, we learn and each day with you no matter how

bitter, it's always sweet to hear your voice, and feel your

touch, those shorts you wear that reveal too much, what a

sight to see, to know that you are down for me!

Even I must laugh, at the humor of it all that a woman like

you could bring out the best, to encourage me without

even trying, today you made me mad, and for that I'm

thankful, cause in confusion you motivated me to drop

these lines, to express the way I feel through the power of

my mind.

LuvLock

Poem: Theory of The Reasons As To Why She Refuses To Love

To adjust and adapt to the circumstances can't be explained in mere words, it would take me a lifetime to explain the reality of who you are, because a broken life has crushed you and forced you to rebuild and become a better person, and you find this a struggle, not that you lack independence you want the comfort of true love but you don't want to surrender your heart because you're afraid of the unknown, yet in actuality you continue to deny the Truth, because you'd rather be blind, than to ever see love lost again, and this is what scares me, but even if you never let me enter, just to have been present to know you is a beauty in itself, yet even I in all wisdom seem perplexed as to the reason why she refuses to love!

Poem: In My Rear-view

22 years before this date, Destiny was born

as I learned my fate. Accelerate pass foes,

as they attempt to capture my license plate

In a hot pursuit of deadly fire, my hands feel like steel

as I balance control of the wheel and tire.

Death on my tail, not trying dying and I refuse to go to jail

Petal to the metal, hydroplaning down memory lane

I see the boy I use to be, so humble and sweet,

he helps the old lady across the street

Yes ma'am and no ma'am he would politely say,

the elders at church wondered

how he could turn out this way

No mother to cry she had long since been dead,

no father to blame his soul was to enchained

but unlike like him I was still physically free,

at least for the moment

LuvLock

Running out of time, the road thins, sirens blare one

officer on the speaker says " Pull over right there"

After they ran my record they were sorely confused as to

why I ran, the lieutenant said

he had no crimes on the man!

We run because we fear your tactics a brother said,

we run because we have no due process of law another

said, and the kid they thought dead arose from the gurney

as the last spoke and he said "I ran because I saw an officer

placed drugs on my friend, I ran because of what I saw at

the age of ten, they killed Roundtree he was only 16 then,

so on this assumption I figured they would kill me too" the

boy closed his eyes taking one last look at the life

he once knew, as all around him became darkness

and the sky turned a dark hue!

LuvLock

Poem: Quid-Pro-Quo

Now that I've gained your attention,

I can see it clearly now that you've been listening

Just sit back and watch me fulfill your dreams,

as I pour the whip cream

The bedroom goes boom, each time I go down

it's like I'm loading the clips, with each burst

you moan a sweet sound

Before I ever touched you I made your knees weak,

and on that day we speak, I mean spoke I didn't choke

Babe you've got me feenin like I'm high on dope,

I just hope;

That this never ends, you don't seem to be cruel, yes

believe I'm no fool went get caught hanging by a rope

I can see the future it's a wonderful view, if you wondering

why I'm hustling, don't trip because I hustle for you

Each time we step out it's all eyes on you, character and

content it's all virtuous

Prince Ami | 86

LuvLock

There's no word to explain, the way you drive me crazy

except insane And it's funny how you say my name,

but babe I like it nonetheless I will give you my all,

if you'll give me your best

Poem: Moving On

It's a continuous warfare out here starving for love,

as if it's my last meal

My heart thumps for her like she my quick fix,

intercepted my heart another pick six

My inner instincts, are telling me there's a sick twist

Inhale on my baby Ms. Mary when I need comfort

she never fails me,

keeps a brother spirit feeling well and healthy

I'm looking for you lady

thinking how sweet you used to be,

these days she seldom home

isn't she supposed to be here to comfort me?

Ultimately it was so kinky and freaky,

each time we did it intimately

So silly I should have knew better than to get entangled in

a love song but now that love's gone, I think we should be

grownups and move on!

LuvLock

Poem: In Time & Memory

Dedicated To: Stephanie

In time, I ask will our love surpass the evening's light or shall it evaporate as the morning dew? Even I in all wisdom perplexed and awed, wonder how a humble gent like myself could capture a beauty as rare as you.
Like a gem, among rubble you flourish as no other, making me better, as a nourishment to my soul, each day you renew me continuously to make me whole.
Physically, mentally and spiritually, we have enabled each other to be courageous, as we tackle life's problems together, in a united effort to make each other better.
Succeeding the test of time, you have become the apple of my eye, of your fruit I have pledged to eat, and if time shall end there shall be no doubt I will love you faithfully recreating time in the hereafter so that we may begin a new chapter.
In time and memory!

LuvLock

Poem: Building Blocks

I'll be gentle with your body, I'll be kinky if you'll promise me to be naughty
I'll get straight to the point excuse me if I'm to blunt, baby this is more than sex this is only the beginning of a taste with no time to waste I suggest we begin the race
You and I seems like we finally made it, so elated We got this head start on graduation, from friends to lovers, now we are inseparable from each other
Who would have knew, as the sky's stood blue, on that night I would find a power so true in a woman like you
All the virtue you possess are too many to name, on the date I met you my life was changed
Now I am you and you are me, we'll pass this baton to our young black seeds, and in the history books there will lie our legacy for the world to read.

Poem: Romeo's Lost Letter to Juliet

To be, exist, to mean more to me than myself alone, could

such a feeling exist in this world?

If so could it be unknown to mortal men and women,

whom with eyes may see, and ears might hear, but cannot

tell the feelings of their own hearts.

If the birds sing and the Jasmine's sweet nectar pollinate

before our eyes, will you believe then that this love was

sent from the heaven's above?

LuvLock

Poem: Picture Perfect

Did you ever dream, of a world where everything is evergreen?
It's seems we chase our dreams until we lose everything!
Holding on to sanity by a light string, who would have pictured us making it this far? It was unseen.
Can we picture perfect, if we never capture the picture?
The only time we find peace is when we fall asleep, when we awake it's another day of misery, I believe in us let's chase our goals until we rewrite history.
And in the event I fail I want you to remember me, keep the dream alive by being the person you was meant to be!

LuvLock

Poem: To Question Prophecy

Today someone asked how did you know you would win?

Then I replied, isn't it so written within?

The very core of my flesh, inside the inner parts of my

mind, there's no mistake this was all by design;

Time after time, while others failed, the steps to success I

scaled.

Step by step, day by day, I won because it was meant to be

that way!

LuvLock

Poem: Real Friends

If I had no advice to give because I'm lost for words, no money to contribute because I'm strapped for change, no time to spare because I'm going through some things; would you still have my back? OR might it be that with slack an ease what was once a friendship die as with a horrible disease?

Real Friends never disperse, they'll support you mentally, physically, spiritually and or financially from the cradle to the Hearse, through the good times and worst!

Poem: If You're Alone

You can always confide in me,

to see you're sad makes me so too

To know your pain triggers me with anger,

to know that I can't help my friend when she's in danger;

Whether it be mentally or physically I would like to protect

her from all harm and any threat, I just want you to know

this fact whenever you need a ear I'm always here

To genuinely listen to your complaints and give you all my

love without restraints

LuvLock

Poem: Awoken

Awake I have been awoken by a burning desire
more magical than the sight of the light of day,
only you could inspire me to feel this way,
that I would give up a sense to experience a sense of you,
but what might I trade if I give my sight it would leave me
out of sight with you, if I give the sense of touch
I will no longer be able to feel your ebony skin softly
enveloping mine, maybe I would prefer to be blind,
or rather I should trade taste and scent
but how else would I be able to take in the fragrance of a
goddess whose lips drips of honey dew, I would give my
heart, to embrace your heart.
To know that I have fulfilled my part,
well played as the curtains close, the crowd screams
it's bravos and encores as we both bow graciously
before the throne of Yah where you become mine and I
become yours for better or worse, didn't even rehearse
caught you unexpectedly how being much younger I was
so well versed, I've had my share of wine's in this lifetime,

but only you could quench my thirst until the end of time…..

LuvLock

Poem: My Goalz

My Goalz are 2 not Say Can't Cause I Know I Can, everybody kick it wit you not your friend, don't hold it inside express the way you feel, how you gonna be the man you can't keep it real?

Stay away from the fake's just because you have one bad day doesn't mean you should give up on always

Keep your head up on this route to getting your bread up, I know them haters going to be fed up, I see ya looking you ain't scaring nothing, 3rd Eye stay jumping acrobatic

To set forth and accomplish my goals is a milestone for me and my family and of course I do this for my friends and family

Who support me to keep me standing, stay true never abandon your ambitions to be free, and realize this one fact the only entity holding me back is me, open your mind to realistic possibilities for wealth mentally, physically,

LuvLock

spirituality and financially are you understanding me? With all that said I want be weak that just not in me Goal Getter's just don't go easy.....

Poem: Change of Heart

You use to be my heartbeat, nowadays we don't speak,

I wonder where it went wrong?

Just listen to my heart's song

Tell me if it feel wrong, whatever it takes to make it right,

I'll pay that price,

twice If you slip and fall I'll forever be your crutch, if it's do

or die 10 toes down wit the 40 in the clutch

If they bursting at you then they bursting at us, they don't

want war you can trust

Baby I'll never be mayor, but no ballot could take away

the fact that I actually care about you and your welfare.....

LuvLock

Poem: Smile

Watching someone so strong battle a fight with old age, the wrinkles defines the joys and woes of her life's page, being slowly ripped apart, first her strength then her voice, her ability to reason and make a choice.....

Tears can't explain this undesirable pain of seeing someone so special to me in pain, her smile could break any man of change from his hand, to see her beauty blonder is a horrible thought to ponder, to know you'll be leaving leaves me void, who else will understand my problems and make me merry when I'm bored..... Everything has it's time I never thought it would come for you, But G'ma no matter what I will always smile for You.....

LuvLock

Poem: A Day for Mothers

It was the most beautiful day ever known, at the moment

and time when you were born.

To conceive such a thought as a seed that into this world

you would become and be,

A Lily among thorns you rose against all odds, I watched

you fulfill the responsibilities of a man, when no one else

understood you always had the train of thought to

understand.

It was with you that I transformed from a boy to a Man,

you watched me struggle and bump my head, when I was

hungry my mouth you fed.

No words could explain the feelings

I'll have for you as long as I'm living, the reasons I love you

are too many to number,

but to know it's true you don't have to wonder.

Only you could inspire me to new heights, from my rib

you became Woman, and from your womb I became Man.

LuvLock

When I saw you it was an occurrence more radiant that the sight of light, to open my eyes and become a part of life, in your eye's I found life without you I would have no life, I love you Mama and thanks for paying the ultimate price.

Tru

LuvLock

Poem: Kingston

There are no words to express the anger I feel, a wound cut so deep no amount of time might heal.....
You were sleeping soundly as Mama stepped in, I'll be back in a moment she whispers to hear promising king, she leaves the car running because she know it won't be to long before they're back on the road and safely home.....
But unbeknownst savages lurked, and to this child they had plan's to do dirt, A Mother's cries could be heard throughout the street's the day she wept, many who lost feelings learned to cry again for this child with prayers to the sky, So much pain brought to the human eye.....
To see you go, was the most tragic day, no one could have imagined it would end this way, you finally got your wing's just know in my heart you will always Reign Supreme!

R.I.H Lil Kingston

LuvLock

Poem: The Worst

A baby I think you're the worst,

you're the water to my thirst

I need you like every hook need's a verse, we converse

Late Night, or under the candlelight

Paparazzi flash, just watching her and that ass

Sexy Black 5'7 ready to smash

But we in different time zones, they must have got my

time wrong she there waiting on me to phone home

She laced her letter's with lipstick and perfume and mine

with cologne sincerely James that's my legal name, ain't

got nothing but love for you your Eddie Kane when she

sings to me it's Etta James she clings to me I'm her

everything

Inside my mind I picture us inside a picture frame I give

you the spirit of life to live this life, without you in life

there is no life

LuvLock

These words are so much more than paper, my heart bleeds every word onto this paper…..

If I could go back then turn back the hands of time, this world we live in would all be mine

There would be no need, so there will be no greed I'll be the perfect father to my unborn seed

They done classified me labeled me wrong, redeeming my soul through these here words in this poem

"Only God Can Judge Me" you don't have to love me

I love myself, ain't going to waste my breath by crying for help I'm a warrior till death

Whenever death should play its part, it will never be able to explain the way I feel in my heart, if you could feel his heart then you will know that it's hard

But P.S. to all those on the B.S., no Redress

I'm "Bout It, Bout It" like Master P and No Limit Soulja's,

I'm super gassed hyped up like I been drinking Folgers'

But hold on good morning baby the worst is over…..

LuvLock

Poem: I'm Ready

The Sky's the limit the seeds already sown,

you can feel the vibrations of my heartbeat in this poem.

Can you imagine a world without me and you putting on,

catching vibes just through communications on the

telephone

Feeling's that you inspire cannot be duplicated,

each time I hear your voice they are recreated

I got you so elated

As if you done been faded by a higher power,

watching you finger your pussy while you up in the shower

It's a Kodak moment watching you foreplay kissing your

soft lips rubbing your back down, not going to back down

I'm hoping that you're ready because I couldn't be more

ready than a Soulja that's cornered

so come on babe quit your running

Poem: Farewell

I could have asked for more, but all I wanted was her.

The thrill of chasing or was it just time being wasted

The difficulty of coming to terms,

releasing the most beautiful thing

ever known from your arms Knowing that her fragile heart

couldn't weather such a storm

You endure, in hopes that in due time what was once

unclean would become pure,

Yet uncertainty lurks beyond her hearts dwellings,

maybe she'll stay maybe she won't ain't no telling

Watching her leave, it was at that moment in time

I began to breathe

I can't remember if it was fall or winter,

you took my heart in May and I lost yours in December

Before I set sail, I enjoyed the moments we shared I bid

you farewell....

LuvLock

Poem: The Beginning to an End

How hatred begins in a relationship it first starts

when we become judgmental of our significant others and

start to point out their faults instead of realizing

we have problems of our own and that we've made

mistakes in life too, because no one is perfect!

Instead of realizing the consequences of our actions

we begin to act like it doesn't matter,

when you know it do, but deep down inside

you're afraid to express the way you really feel because

you're afraid they might not understand and this fear of

the unknown is what makes it so hard

for the relationship to rebound.

In your hardest times you forgot to stick together because

you could only think of yourself,

what makes relationship's crumble!

LuvLock

Poem: Complex Feelings

You are complex, not too complex

that I can't figure you out;

it's not your complexion which puzzles me,

because your skin is the same color as mine,

it's just we are conflicted by separation through

desperation our hearts intertwined to mend,

countless nights our hearts would cry away

our struggles one to the other,

we felt a kinship as a sister would to a brother!

An in these facts lies the truth of the matter as to why we

can't be or why we refuse to see what we were destined

to be because in all honesty we are only humans

and with an eye not belonging to I,

a Mortal Man penned these words to describe a feeling

he dares not utter!

Yet inscribed in these unknown words lies deep feelings

only a Goddess could inspire but my lips dare not utter

LuvLock

unless it be that time expires.

Yet let it be so that all be well I would prefer to be

perplexed in a state of awe, love is too complex so he

graciously bows! And to this act The Goddess Smiles......

LuvLock

Poem: Something Special

The greatest gift ever known to man she gave herself up, and by giving her soul to me to uplift me to light she gave me life. Through her I became life into my life she became wife the queen to my heart from beginning to the end the greatest gift ever known to Mankind.....

"Woman"

LuvLock

Poem: Time

Time is only a segment within our own minds,

to acknowledge that something is old only confirms that

we must create something new or redefine what's old into

something better- Food4Thought

About the Author

"LuvLock: is a collection of poems Author Prince Ami wrote over many years. He poured his heart into every word. Although he is not much of a talker, he has found it easier to express himself through his poetry. From as early at the age of 13, writing has become a way for him to demonstrate his intelligence and a means to vent when angry, cry when sad, and experience happiness even when no one else is around.

Prince Ami has all of his love locked inside the words he writes, hence the title *"LuvLock"*.

His reason for publishing his work is so that all the love he has in his heart will be able to flow freely throughout the hearts and minds of each reader!

Poetry Fly Books

Is an imprint of

The Butterfly Typeface Publishing.

Contact us for all your

publishing & writing needs!

Iris M Williams

PO Box 56193

Little Rock AR 72215

www.ingramcontent.com/pod-product-compliance
Lightning Source LLC
Chambersburg PA
CBHW071731090426
42738CB00011B/2457